Let's Eat!

SUSTAINABLE FOOD FOR A HUNGRY PLANET

KIMBERLEY VENESS

ORCA BOOK PUBLISHERS

Library and Archives Canada Cataloguing in Publication

Veness, Kimberley, 1989-, author
Let's eat : sustainable food for a hungry planet / Kimberley Veness.

(Orca footprints)

Includes bibliographical references and index.
Issued in print and electronic formats.
ISBN 978-1-4598-0939-0 (hardcover).—ISBN 978-1-4598-0940-6 (pdf).—
ISBN 978-1-4598-0941-3 (epub)

1. Sustainable agriculture—Juvenile literature. 2. Food supply—
Juvenile literature. I. Title. II. Series: Orca footprints

s494.5.s86v46 2017   j630   c2016-904462-9
          c2016-904463-7

First published in the United States, 2017
Library of Congress Control Number: 2016949028

Summary: Part of the nonfiction Footprints series for middle readers.
Illustrated with many color photographs, this book explores where the food
we eat comes from and what the future of farming looks like.

*A boy selling watermelon at a market in
the capital city of Managua, Nicaragua.*
SJORS737/DREAMSTIME.COM

*Orca Book Publishers is dedicated to preserving the environment and has
printed this book on Forest Stewardship Council® certified paper.*

Orca Book Publishers gratefully acknowledges the support for
its publishing programs provided by the following agencies:
the Government of Canada through the Canada Book Fund and the
Canada Council for the Arts, and the Province of British Columbia
through the BC Arts Council and the Book Publishing Tax Credit.

Cover images by Getty Images, Shari Nakagawa
Back cover images (top left to right): Fallen Fruit (David Burns
and Austin Young), Kiva, Helder Ramos; (bottom left to right):
William Neumann Photography, Katie Stagliano,
William Neumann Photography

ORCA BOOK PUBLISHERS
www.orcabook.com

Printed and bound in Canada.

20 19 18 17 • 4 3 2 1

For my children, Landon and Sawyer

Contents

CHAPTER ONE:
LET'S EAT!

CHAPTER TWO:
SMALL IS BEAUTIFUL

CHAPTER THREE: URBAN FOODSCAPES

CHAPTER FOUR: A FARM FOR THE FUTURE

Introduction

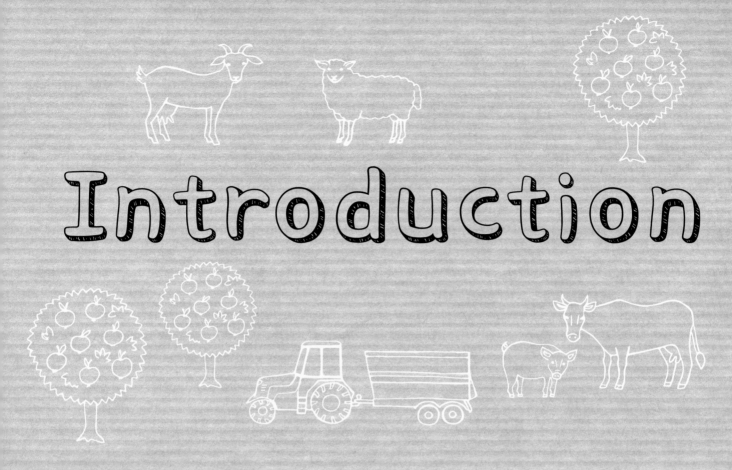

My son Landon and I picking apples at an orchard in Kelowna, British Columbia. One of his first foods was applesauce I made with apples from this orchard. Now he will happily devour a whole apple in one sitting, core and all! LAURA CARBONNEAU

Do you ever wonder what your groceries would tell you if they could talk? When I realized that the bananas, avocados and mandarin oranges I loved had traveled across more countries than I ever had, I decided to pay closer attention to where my food came from. I discovered that everything you buy, whether it's an apple or a pair of shoes, has a story. I found out my salmon fillet came from a fish that had never swum in the ocean, my orange juice was previously brown, and some ingredients in my favorite packaged foods had originated from plants conceived under a microscope! This book unlocks the mysterious secret lives of our groceries, explores alternative—and sometimes bizarre—farm technology, and tours gardens up high on corporate rooftops to down low in military-style bunkers beneath city streets.

Few children in North America are growing up to become farmers like their parents and grandparents before them. SUSAN H. SMITH/ISTOCK.COM

From Farm to Table

When I was a child, my family lived on a farm in Saskatchewan. I loved planting, watering and harvesting veggies, helping my mom make jams and pies from Saskatoon berries, collecting chicken eggs and drinking milk fresh from our cow, Daisy, and goat, Pixie. Now that I'm a mom, I try to find the healthiest foods for my family and make as much as I can from scratch with whatever's in the fridge or pantry.

This is me herding our three goats and cow, led by the rope, up to the barn.
KIMBERLEY VENESS

CHAPTER ONE

Let's Eat

Seasonal produce is available year-round at most grocery stores. TOLGAILDUN/DREAMSTIME.COM

When you push the cart around the grocery store with your mom or dad, do you ever stop and think about where all the food comes from? The answer may surprise you.

A VEGGIE MARATHON

If you're shopping in North America, your groceries may travel between 2,400 and 4,000 kilometers (1,500 and 2,500 miles) before you actually eat them. Getting food from another country seems like an outlandish idea when you could find fresh options closer to home, but products grown in other countries are often cheaper because of lower labor costs and fewer *environmental regulations*. Farm workers are often underpaid and forced to live and work in poor conditions. Buying local reduces transport time and supports the local economy, but farmers in cooler climates can't grow heat-loving crops like strawberries year-round. So what do you do? Do you add a box of imported strawberries to your cart or wait for local strawberries to come back in season?

Locals peruse the produce at this market in Ahmedabad, India. MANANSHAH1008/WIKIPEDIA.ORG

IN EXCESS WE TRUST

Imagine you're walking down a gravel road in the Canadian prairies. Canola (a crop that is processed into canola oil and used worldwide in cooking) grows on both sides of the road, covering the land in a bright yellow blanket as far as the eye can see. It's beautiful, but it comes at a price. Agriculture has come a long way from the postcard picture of a cozy farmhouse, a red barn and fields planted with a variety of crops. Few of our foods originate from farms like these. Most of the berries, fruit, veggies and grains we eat come from *monocultures*—single crops grown on large areas of land. Growing just one crop makes harvest and pest management much easier for farmers who grow on a large scale.

Before the *Industrial Revolution*, when machines started to replace human labor, farmers relied on planting and harvesting with the aid of horses or oxen, and sometimes help from family members and neighbors. School even let out earlier in the afternoon around harvest time so children could lend a hand. Prior to 1834, when the first reaper (a machine for cutting down grain) hit the market, grain crops were harvested by hand with a sickle (a handheld tool with a curved blade), and it could take weeks for one farmer to harvest his field of grain, even with extra help.

Workers picked these beans in the morning, and customers will pick them up in the afternoon. SOL KAUFFMAN

FARMING FACT: Did you know that digging your hands into a garden bed has been scientifically proven to increase happiness? Gardeners touch and breathe in a soil bacterium called *Mycobacterium vaccae*, which stimulates the feel-good sensors in the brain.

Farmers harvesting by hand.
LC-DIG-MATPC-14346/LIBRARY OF CONGRESS

Before machines, farmers used plows to break up the soil on their fields. Horses had to be specially trained for the job, and it was slow, exhausting work.
75-RBD-560/NATIONAL ARCHIVES

FARMING FACT: In 1988, the United States produced nearly 5 million bushels of corn, harvesting about 85 bushels per acre from 58,250 acres of cropland. Think that's a lot of corn? In the 2010 to 2011 harvest year, the United States produced nearly 12.5 million bushels of corn, harvesting about 155 bushels per acre from 81.4 million acres of cropland. Increased fertilizer and pesticide use and expansion of cropland has made yields skyrocket.

Now, almost two hundred years later, it takes only hours. The first combine (grain-harvesting machine) was created in 1835 and came into use in the United States around 1900, and its successors can seed fields, add fertilizer and pesticides, and harvest crops with unparalleled efficiency. But does speed and efficiency produce the best possible food, and how has speeding up food production changed what we know about what we eat?

FULL CIRCLE

When I was a child, I used to think the thirty-minute drive that separated my town from the nearest city meant the two places were completely unconnected. I learned later that the entire Earth is one giant *ecosystem* connected by wind and water. The *chemical fertilizers* and *pesticides* sprayed on huge monoculture farms accumulate in clouds and fall elsewhere in rain. They run off fields into streams and contaminate waterways and plants and animals—the same ones we may harvest or hunt. These chemicals can take a long time to break down in the environment, accumulating in our bodies and in the atmosphere. Agricultural emissions alone add more greenhouse gases to the atmosphere than all of the planes, trains and motor vehicles in the world combined. That McDonald's burger-and-fries combo you may enjoy once a week could be worse for Earth's air quality than the exhaust from your parents' car on the drive to buy your burger.

OUR DAILY MEAT

If you were living in Mesopotamia (modern-day Turkey, Iraq, Iran and Syria) about 8,000 years ago, you might have been one of the first people to domesticate farm animals. The newly settled nomads, who had started cultivating crops a few thousand years earlier, fenced off large portions of land and captured wild herds of goats, sheep and, later, pigs and cattle. Farmers

Farmers in Maryland, threshing grain from the chaff. The bags of grain will then be taken to the mill to be ground. LOCKE, EDWIN/LIBRARY OF CONGRESS

could better predict how much meat they would have to eat, trade or sell if they were able to keep track of all the animals. Settling down and raising livestock provided more security than hunting, leaving more time to expand farms and families.

All livestock in today's *Concentrated Animal Feeding Operations* (CAFOs), where the majority of meat sold in grocery stores comes from, are descendants of those first domesticated animals. Ninety-nine percent of livestock in the United States is CAFO-raised. Over the decades, costs for livestock, feed, antibiotics and veterinary care have increased by leaps and bounds, and the meat industry has had to expand to cut costs. Like monocultures, CAFOs focus on getting the product from start to store as fast as possible. Many CAFO-raised animals seldom see the light of day, and some never do. A chicken may spend its entire life in a cage smaller than a microwave.

Cows fed grass their whole lives can take up to twenty-four months to reach slaughter weight, while cows in *feedlots* (CAFOs for cows raised for beef) reach that weight as early as fourteen months, gaining one to two kilograms (two to four pounds) a day. The efficiency with which feedlot cows gain weight is the number one reason why 95 percent of cows raised for beef in the United States spend the final months of their lives in feedlots.

Many of the 1.5 billion domesticated cows on earth spend their first six months at pasture before being transported to feedlots, the cattle version of a CAFO. DAVID HUGHES/ISTOCK.COM

Most animals love to socialize and forage in open spaces. If they can't act on these natural instincts, they can become stressed and develop harmful behaviors. SOL KAUFFMAN

FARMING FACT: Eating krill (a tiny shrimp-like crustacean) turns the flesh of wild salmon bright pink-orange. Farmed salmon are fed a synthetic enzyme that dyes their flesh a pinkish hue. It still isn't as bright as wild salmon, but without it farmed salmon would look gray.

CHEAP NOW, COSTLY LATER

When compared to the price of meat from an animal raised at pasture, the meat from a CAFO animal is less expensive in the store. But while the price tag to the consumer—you and me—may be low, the environmental cost, in the form of the massive amount of land and water required to grow the feed for the animals, and the toxic sewage that often seeps out of a feedlot into nearby lakes, streams and rivers, is high.

Imagine arriving at your favorite lake for a swim. You see a sign that says high levels of chemicals in the lake now make it unsafe for swimmers. The next time you visit the lake you may see another advisory sign that says the fish in the lake are not safe to eat. Water *contamination* is a real problem, but, thankfully, environmental groups and committed citizens work hard to protect these fragile ecosystems.

A satellite orbiting earth snapped this photo of a Texas feedlot. Each rectangular area holds hundreds of cows. Their waste pools in the center of the feedlot. MISHKA HENNER, COURTESY BRUCE SILVERSTEIN GALLERY, NY

A worker feeds the fish at this fish farm in Thailand. SUKPAIBOONWAT/SHUTTERSTOCK.COM

AQUACULTURE: A FISH FOR EVERYONE

When commercial capture fishing was booming in the 1940s and 1950s, most finfish (fish with fins) were double, sometimes triple, the size they are today. Nowadays, fishermen often catch fish before they reach full size. Some species of rockfish can live for 150 years! They take twenty years to reach reproductive maturity, so if they cannot reproduce before fishermen haul them aboard a ship, no younger fish are born to take their place in the food chain. Such overfishing has depleted wild fish stocks, turning the world's focus to fish farming or aquaculture.

More than 600 aquatic species are raised through aquaculture—half of all seafood consumed by people today. Most of the production happens in Asia, where seafood is a staple in people's diets and a key *export commodity*. Fisheries provide jobs for millions of people all over the world. In China, more than fourteen million people work as fishers or fish farmers.

Finfish

Tilapia, carp, trout and Atlantic salmon are all common farmed finfish species. Farm-raised salmon eat dry pellets made from fish meal, fish oil and veggie products. The meal and oil used in aquaculture feed comes from small fish that travel in large schools. Some people believe raising vegetarian or omnivorous fish like tilapia, which prefer to eat algae, is better because their food doesn't require removing other animals from the food chain.

Aquaculture of marine finfish usually happens in open-net pens in the ocean, but these farms can devastate the surrounding environment and sea life. Fish waste causes toxic algae blooms that suck oxygen from the water. Disease and parasites like sea lice spread quickly inside the crowded pens and can infect wild migrating salmon.

In the last decade, commercial aquaculture has started moving from ocean to land. Supporters of on-land aquaculture

Chew on This!

PAMELAJOEMCFARLANE/ISTOCK.COM

Make a list of everything you eat for one day, including snacks. Look at the food package or sticker and write down which country the item came from. By the end of the day you may be surprised by how well-traveled your food is! If you want to go a step further, compare lists with friends to see who has the most local food in their diet, or go online and google the distance between the capital cities of the countries where your food came from and the city where you live. Add up the food miles. The combined distance might be enough to circle the Earth—more than once!

say it's the more environmentally sustainable option. Fish live in tanks with no risk of transmitting diseases to wild salmon, and no risk of escapees competing with native marine life. They require less protein in their feed because they expend less energy. And when their waste is filtered and processed, it even makes a rich fertilizer for gardens.

Invertebrates

Animals without a backbone are called *invertebrates*, and we share the world with millions of them, from ants and bees to shellfish and jellyfish. Mollusks (like mussels and oysters) and arthropods (like shrimp and prawns) are popular aquaculture invertebrates. Mollusks have been around for 500 million years, and arthropods make up over 75 percent of all animal species in the world!

Woodblock depicting a woman toasting a sheet of nori over an open fire, Japan, 1864.
BENICHAN/WIKIPEDIA.ORG

From Farm to Table

In my home province of British Columbia, salmon is a keystone species sacred to First Nations people. Through every stage of their lives, wild salmon provide an essential food source for well over a hundred species, from seagulls to eagles, otters to orcas, wolves to grizzly bears, humans and more. Sadly, warming water temperatures, the construction of hydro-electric dams, and parasites from farmed salmon continue to reduce the number of salmon returning to spawn.

Salmon turn bright red when spawning.
MURPHY_SHEWCHUK/ISTOCK.COM

Aquatic Plants and Algae

Aquatic plants, such as different types of seaweed and algae feed herbivorous or omnivorous farmed fish. For some people, eating seaweed is as normal as eating potato chips. If you like sushi, you have probably snacked on rolls wrapped in nori. This seaweed is a staple food in Japan, dating back over 1,300 years! Its value was so high, it was sometimes used as currency. In 2012, about eight billion kilograms (nine million tons) of seaweed was farmed to feed people, mostly in East Asia.

WHAT'S YOUR FOOD REALLY SAYING?

More people are seeking out meat and seafood from animals raised under humane and sustainable conditions. Yet even with this push for better food, loose labeling regulations leave it to the consumer to do the homework and figure out where their food comes from, and what it is. The following charts will help you identify the most healthful foods.

FARMING FACT: It takes 1.4 kilograms (3 pounds) of feed for a farmed salmon to gain 1 kilogram (2 pounds), and about 5.4 kilograms (12 pounds) of feed for a feedlot cow to gain 1 kilogram.

SEAFOOD

SeaChoice, an organization dedicated to identifying sustainable seafood, uses a traffic light-color system to make it easy for consumers to choose sustainable seafood.

Green
The seafood was sustainably caught and the population is stable.

Yellow
There are problems with the seafood's fishery, whether it's unsustainable fishing practices or conservation concerns, and it's recommended you don't eat it often.

Red
There are multiple problems with the fishery and with conservation efforts. The seafood may be endangered, and it's recommended you don't eat the seafood until it receives a better ranking.

These ranchers are herding their cattle on horseback, a job the whole family can take part in. STEVEN ALLAN/ISTOCK.COM

BEEF

Buying humanely raised beef may cost more, yet every time someone chooses humanely raised over feedlot raised, they support a healthier food system, now and in the future.

100% grass-fed
The cow's diet consisted of strictly grass, so it probably spent much of its life at pasture.

Grass-finished
The cow probably had access to pasture and its diet consisted primarily of grass, but it may have occasionally been fed some grain.

Grass-fed
The cow probably had access to pasture and ate grass, but was probably fed corn, grain or *animal by-products* during the last few months of its life to gain weight fast. This is also sometimes called grain-finished.

Organic
If the label is USDA Organic, the cow could still have lived in a feedlot. It ate organic feed and did not eat animal by-products or receive antibiotics or *growth hormones*.

Naturally raised
The cow could still have lived in a feedlot. It probably ate corn, grain and animal by-products and received frequent doses of antibiotics and growth hormones.

A, AA or AAA beef
The cow had similar diet and living conditions as the naturally-raised cow. The difference between the A, AA or AAA depends on marbling or distribution of fat.

FRUITS AND VEGETABLES

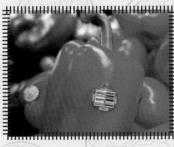

You can tell this pepper was conventionally grown by the four numbers on the sticker beginning with the number four. RYAN LAUZE

You're used to peeling the sticker off your apple before you wash and eat it, but did you know that the numbers on that sticker tell a story? As we get more efficient at producing food, we need to make sure we are equally efficient at maintaining a sustainable food system for the future. Food labels can help us make informed decisions.

Organically grown
Stickers have five digits and start with the number 9.

Conventionally grown
Stickers have four digits and start with the number 3 or 4.

Genetically modified organism (GMO)
Stickers have five digits and start with the number 8.

CHAPTER TWO

Small Is Beautiful

When I was a kid, my siblings and I loved to climb hay bales and survey our farmland. That was our house in the background.
KIMBERLEY VENESS

Not every farmer thinks huge monocultures and CAFOs are the right way to farm. So what are the alternatives? In this chapter, we'll take a tour of farming techniques that favor a smaller scale and are more sustainable in their approach.

Most people in North America garden for pleasure, but in other parts of the world, maintaining a prosperous garden is more than a hobby—it's a necessity. Over 570 million farms exist worldwide and more than 90 percent are owned and worked by families. These family farms are responsible for over 80 percent of global food production. Most are in developing countries and are a little under one hectare, or about the size of two football fields. Work is often still done by hand, and if they can afford to go to school at all, children may get out of school early to help their parents on the farm.

ON THE HOMESTEAD

If you were a European settling North America in the 1600-1800s, you and your family might have crossed the continent in a horse-drawn wagon, searching for a place to call home. Imagine what it must have been like to live so far from civilization, with only your immediate family for company. You would have to be pretty skilled to survive without outside help, much like the indigenous people who lived in North America ten thousand years before the first Europeans set foot on the land.

People who choose to, or have to, live with limited resources and outside help have accumulated a cache of knowledge that allows them to grow food, raise and care for animals, build shelters and use medicinal plants to cure the sick. It's not an easy life! I have heard people call living off the land in this way "simple" living, but there is nothing simple about it!

Some homesteaders capture rainwater to drink and use solar panels to harvest the sun's energy to power lights and small

This pioneer family was traveling west through Loup Valley, Nebraska, with all their belongings in order to find suitable farmland in 1886.
NATIONAL ARCHIVES/ARCHIVES.GOV

FARMING FACT: Of the 319 million people living in the United States, only 1 percent are farmers.

From Farm to Table

I love quinoa, and it's super easy to grow. Our garden on Vancouver Island was about the size of a backyard swimming pool, complete with a 2-meter-tall (7-foot-tall) deer fence with large stones around the base to keep the wild rabbits from burrowing under. The tall, colorful buds of quinoa rested lazily on the top of the fence. Thankfully, the natural bitter coating of the quinoa seed took it off the menu for the deer.

Processing quinoa takes some time. You have to roll out the grains from their casings, strain the plant matter, rinse multiple times and set the grains aside to dry. KIMBERLEY VENESS

19

On Mongolia's windswept plateaus, vegetation is scarce. Families with cattle herds are constantly on the move, searching for new grazing grounds. This woman in Mongolia is processing milk from her cattle.
ALEKSANDR FROLOV/DREAMSTIME.COM

Chew on This!

HJALMEIDA/ISTOCK.COM

Find out where there are farms in your area and contact them to see if you can schedule a visit. Sometimes farmers hire volunteers for one-time group tasks, like weeding or harvesting, where you can spend a full day as a farmhand and maybe even get to take home some yummy veggies you picked yourself. Fruits and vegetables are most nutritious just after they are picked, and plants grown in healthy soil produce the tastiest and most nutrient-packed food. Fresh is best!

appliances, while others drink from clean freshwater streams and wake and sleep on the sun's schedule. Could you imagine never seeing water spill from the tap into your bathtub, or not being able to flick the light on if it were too dark to see?

WORK IT

When you live on a farm, something always needs doing. Many farmers have a range of skills, which lets them cut costs by handling farm jobs by themselves. Nowadays, agricultural land, animal feed and vaccines, and even the animals themselves are more expensive, so cutting costs is essential for small farmers, who may not be bringing in a steady income.

NEW ROOTS

If you were a country kid growing up sixty years ago, there was a good chance you would have inherited your parent's farm and become a farmer too—many children in developing countries still do that today. This all changed over the last few decades in developed countries, with young adults opting for higher education or jobs in the city, making the average age of farmers in North America fifty-five or older. Rising costs make it difficult for aspiring farmers to tap into the industry, now dominated by industrial-sized farms.

Nevertheless, many young people are learning all they can about agriculture in the hopes of starting their own farm. Volunteer programs like WWOOF (World Wide Opportunities

FARMING FACT: Some farmers use a technique called *lasagna gardening*, and as with good lasagna, everyone has their own recipe. Stacking layers of compostable scraps, coffee grounds, leaves, straw and newspaper clippings on top of the garden creates rich, healthy soil and requires zero digging or tilling!

A girl holding freshly picked guavas in Bamako, Mali.
COMMERCEANDCULTURESTOCK/GETTY IMAGES

Chew on This!

Write down all of the ingredients that make up your favorite sandwich, including the basics like bread and mayonnaise. Now make a list of each item's ingredients. For example, to make bread you would need flour, yeast (or some other leavening agent), cooking oil, salt, sugar and water. Once you finish your list, imagine you are living in the 1800s. To make your favorite sandwich, you would need to grow every ingredient yourself, purchase them at a store, or trade with a neighbor. To get the bread, your family would have to grow the wheat, pound it into flour and bake it on a wood-burning stove. If you're like me and believe no sandwich is complete without pickles, you would have to grow cucumbers and pickle them in vinegar, salt, garlic and dill—which you would have to grow or buy too.

on Organic Farms) connect aspiring farmers with existing ones. Volunteers can travel all over the world, learning the different agriculture practices of each country they visit.

PERMACULTURE

Permaculture is the creation of sustainable, self-sufficient ecosystems for the long term, requiring less input of chemical pesticides, water and human labor, and resulting in less output of greenhouse gases.

Like people, plants are happiest when surrounded by helpful friends. Some plants emit excess nutrients as they grow, which helps their neighbors, while the scents of others ward off pests or attract pollinators. Planting crops with these relationships in mind is called *companion planting*, and it's one of the best ways to ensure healthy plant growth, soil fertility and pest control. It works on any scale, from pots on an apartment patio to a rural farmer's field.

THE 'NO-TILL' ZONE

Tilling the ground is like kicking an anthill. It took a long time for the ants to build the intricate passageways and chambers to make their home functional, and it will take just as long to repair the damage. Like ants, soil microbes take time to build healthy soil. Conventional farming, which over-tills the soil, strips away soil nutrients over time. Because commercial agriculture is all about efficiency, farmers add fertilizers instead of waiting for the soil to regain its natural nutrients. Over time, soil nutrients get so depleted the only way they could come back naturally would be if farming stopped completely for years. When the ground is rarely or never tilled, the microbial community can grow unimpeded, making healthy soil and all but eliminating erosion and the need for additional fertilizer.

RICE-DUCK FARMING

Did you ever think a rice farmer's prized tool might be a gaggle of honking ducks? Centuries-old *integrated rice and duck farming* originated in Japan and is gaining popularity in the Philippines, where the humid, rainy climate is perfect for rice cultivation. Each day, the farmer leads the ducks to the rice paddies. The hungry fowl eat up pests like grasshoppers and snails, and their droppings fertilize the growing rice. At the end of the day, the farmer leads the group back to their coop. Once the ducks are mature, farmers can eat them or sell them for meat.

Rice farmers used ducks to manage pests thousands of years ago before using synthetic pesticides became common practice.
EKATERINA POKROVSKY/DREAMSTIME.COM

ORGANIC OR BUST

Farmers who grow *certified organic* food without using synthetic pesticides or fertilizers may still use pesticides and fertilizers that occur naturally (like copper sulfate, which is used to control tadpole populations in rice paddies), so long as they do not contaminate the plants, soil or water. Certified organic

FARMING FACT: A single non-organic grape or sweet bell pepper contains fifteen different kinds of pesticides.

Some small farms let you pick your own berries! It's a fun way to learn more about where your food comes from if you don't have the space to grow it yourself. JENN PLAYFORD

foods can't come from *genetically modified* seeds and plants, and processed foods labeled "100% Organic" must contain at least 95 percent organic ingredients. Most pesticides accumulate in the skin of fruits and vegetables, so washing and peeling can help reduce the amount of pesticides you eat. Some believe cooking can lower pesticide levels too, but it can also reduce nutrients.

PASTEURIZED VS. RAW

Pasteurization occurs when a product is heated up to extend its shelf life and kill harmful bacteria before it is sold for human consumption. All milk; dairy products like cream, butter, cheese and yogurt; and fruit juices sold in any grocery store have almost certainly been pasteurized.

Pasteurization was invented in 1864, but at the time most people were still getting milk from the family cow on a daily basis. There was little need to extend shelf life if you could slip on your rubber boots, walk out to the barn and squeeze

Bottles of hibiscus and mint kombucha, a fermented tea.
KATHERINE VAN BLYDERVEEN

From Farm to Table

I made butter for the first time a few years ago when I was a member of a cow share. (About ten other people and I paid the feed and veterinary costs for a Jersey cow on a small farm, and in return we received raw milk each week. The milk was so rich the cream formed a two-inch layer on top. I had to shake the jar before drinking!) To make butter, I spooned the cream into a blender and blended on high until it thickened, then put it in cheesecloth and pressed the moisture onto a paper towel.

This homemade butter was so delicious it didn't even need salt!
KIMBERLEY VENESS

enough milk from the cow's udder to fill your glass. Illness from drinking raw cow milk was rare, but when people did get sick, they often died. Pasteurization was put into law in Canada in 1938, around the same time families who had moved from their farms to the suburbs were installing fridges in their kitchens, extending the shelf life of their food. Pasteurization was becoming common in the United States, too, and became law there in 1987. Raw milk has good bacteria that's helpful for digestive health and our immune system, but both beneficial and harmful bacteria are killed off through pasteurization.

FROM FARM TO MARKET

Have you ever been to a farmers' market? They bustle with vendors and shoppers all chattering at once, and a blend of smells permeates the air: spices, drinks and hot-off-the-barbecue burgers made with local beef. Farmers' markets have been around for thousands of years, offering a variety of unique goods produced by local farmers, bakers, artists and artisans.

FARMING FACT: Human waste, called *biosolids*, makes superb fertilizer if it undergoes proper treatment to remove *pathogens* (viruses, bacteria or other microorganisms that cause disease). In the United States, about 50 percent of American biosolids are used to fertilize non-edible plants. Some homesteaders use human waste exclusively to fertilize their gardens.

Vendors dock their food-laden boats in this floating market in Thailand. MANIT LARPLUECHAI/DREAMSTIME.COM

Urban Foodscapes

One hundred years ago, only two out of every ten people lived in cities. Since 2010, that number is up to five, meaning half the world's population now lives in cities—and 60 million more people move to cities each year! Tons of food are trucked, shipped and flown in to keep everyone fed. If a natural disaster struck and transportation halted, stores would run out of food within days. Finding a sustainable and reliable way to feed people who live in cities is one of the biggest problems of our time.

McDonald's serves 68 million customers every day. The company has stores in 118 countries, making it easy for people to grab a filling, but often unhealthy, bite to eat.
VINCENT VAN ZEIJST/WIKIPEDIA.ORG

DO YOU LIVE IN A FOOD DESERT?

If you have no car and don't live within walking distance of a grocery store or market, then you live in what's called a *food desert*. Not the kind of desert with towering sand dunes but one with industrial facilities and suburban neighborhoods. Imagine walking for hours without coming across a grocery store or an outdoor market. Some food deserts have no food retailers at all.

RICE-DUCK FARMING

Did you ever think a rice farmer's prized tool might be a gaggle of honking ducks? Centuries-old *integrated rice and duck farming* originated in Japan and is gaining popularity in the Philippines, where the humid, rainy climate is perfect for rice cultivation. Each day, the farmer leads the ducks to the rice paddies. The hungry fowl eat up pests like grasshoppers and snails, and their droppings fertilize the growing rice. At the end of the day, the farmer leads the group back to their coop. Once the ducks are mature, farmers can eat them or sell them for meat.

Rice farmers used ducks to manage pests thousands of years ago before using synthetic pesticides became common practice.
EKATERINA POKROVSKY/DREAMSTIME.COM

ORGANIC OR BUST

Farmers who grow *certified organic* food without using synthetic pesticides or fertilizers may still use pesticides and fertilizers that occur naturally (like copper sulfate, which is used to control tadpole populations in rice paddies), so long as they do not contaminate the plants, soil or water. Certified organic

FARMING FACT: A single non-organic grape or sweet bell pepper contains fifteen different kinds of pesticides.

Some small farms let you pick your own berries! It's a fun way to learn more about where your food comes from if you don't have the space to grow it yourself. JENN PLAYFORD

Urban Foodscapes

One hundred years ago, only two out of every ten people lived in cities. Since 2010, that number is up to five, meaning half the world's population now lives in cities—and 60 million more people move to cities each year! Tons of food are trucked, shipped and flown in to keep everyone fed. If a natural disaster struck and transportation halted, stores would run out of food within days. Finding a sustainable and reliable way to feed people who live in cities is one of the biggest problems of our time.

DO YOU LIVE IN A FOOD DESERT?

If you have no car and don't live within walking distance of a grocery store or market, then you live in what's called a *food desert*. Not the kind of desert with towering sand dunes but one with industrial facilities and suburban neighborhoods. Imagine walking for hours without coming across a grocery store or an outdoor market. Some food deserts have no food retailers at all.

McDonald's serves 68 million customers every day. The company has stores in 118 countries, making it easy for people to grab a filling, but often unhealthy, bite to eat.
VINCENT VAN ZEIJST/WIKIPEDIA.ORG

Others have fast-food restaurants and convenience stores full of processed food, but no fresh, whole food like fruits and vegetables. So people without cars have to settle for the fatty, sugary options close by.

Food deserts exist all over the developed world, and the people living in them may not have the resources—space, knowledge, time or money—to grow a garden from seed to harvest. Thankfully, cities are taking note of this problem and working with people to set aside spaces for gardens, so everyone can have access to healthy food.

GARDENING TOGETHER

Commons gardens are a great option for people who want to grow fresh food but don't have access to any land where they live. Commons provide an opportunity to learn from other gardeners, harvest healthy crops and share the goodness with others.

FARMING FACT: Twelve percent of land on Earth, more than 1.5 billion hectares (3.7 billion acres), is being used to grow food. That's an area nearly twice the size of Australia, and it's expanding every day.

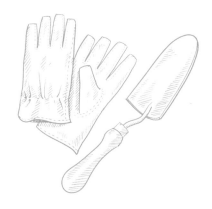

It's never too late to check out what's growing in your neighborhood commons garden! KALI9/ISTOCK.COM

Any passerby can enjoy the bounty of these gardens so long as they follow proper foraging etiquette: never harvest more than you need. There is less chance for waste this way, and you ensure others can harvest too. You can always go back for more in a few days. Be careful not to confuse commons gardens with *community gardens*. In the commons, anyone can work on or harvest from the garden, while community gardeners each purchase a plot within the allotted gardening area and grow, care for and harvest their food independently. You don't want to make the mistake of harvesting the product of someone else's hard work!

FOOD FORESTS

What has multiple levels and food all around? A *food forest* (also known as a forest garden). These permaculture landscapes are not your typical one-level garden. Every plant in a food forest—from tubers to vines to trees—produces something edible at different times of the year.

Once established, food forests are relatively easy to maintain. When trees mature, their deep root system finds water low in the soil, reducing the need for additional watering. The tree canopy casts shade for shade-loving plants. Ground cover crops shield the soil from the sun's hot rays and keep the soil from drying up. During periods of heavy rainfall, their roots hold the soil together to combat erosion, keeping nutrients and microbial life in place for the surrounding plants.

COMMERCIAL URBAN FARMS

Neighborhood food gardens and forests can provide families with good food, but only implementation on a much larger scale could feed a city, and there isn't usually enough urban ground space to expand. Thankfully, commercial urban farms (which

produce and sell food on a large scale) are starting to address this need, and many are using cutting-edge technology to grow food in ways deemed impossible just a few decades ago.

Grow it inside

Unlike conventional farms, which engineer plants to better suit the environment, indoor farms create environments more suited to the plants. Crops grown in a controlled indoor environment are not exposed to seasonal weather changes like storms or early frost. Lighting, water and nutrients are administered in ways finely tuned to yield the best product in the least amount of time.

Most indoor commercial urban farms are powered by LED (light-emitting diode) lights. If you could tell your great-grandparents that people are now eating vegetables that never encountered soil or sunlight, they probably wouldn't believe you.

Located in an abandoned World War II bomb shelter below the streets of London, Urban Underground is the first underground commercial urban farm of its kind.
GROWING UNDERGROUND

From Farm to Table

I walked by Mason Street City Farm in Victoria, British Columbia, probably a hundred times before I realized what it was. One of my university professors took our class on a field trip to visit the quarter-acre farm, smack-dab in the middle of the city, less than a ten-minute walk from the downtown core. The farm feeds a number of families and supplies salad mixes, beans and other crops to local restaurants. They even keep a small flock of chickens who snack on compost and plant clippings.

Rows of greens growing at Mason Street City Farm.
SHARI NAKAGAWA

This 1,400-square-foot hydroponic greenhouse sits on top of a school amidst the skyscrapers of New York City and is just one of the 100 greenhouse labs planned to be in place by 2020. ARI BURLING

The lucky employees at this office building in Tokyo, Japan, get to work alongside lush gardens of veggies—and eat them too! KONO DESIGNS LLC

The first LED light was invented in 1962, and decades later upgraded versions illuminate everything from indoor farms to the flat-screen TV in your living room. The plants are grown using a technique called *hydroponics*, which completely removes soil from the gardening equation. Farmers seed the plants into specialized growing mediums, such as rocks or coconut fiber, or sometimes directly into plastic trays so roots dangle fully submerged in water.

Another indoor farming technique is aeroponics. Roots hang suspended in air and soak up nutrients through mist. Micro and salad greens are the easiest veggies to grow this way, and since this technology is still relatively new, greens are the main products being grown. Micro and salad greens are harvested young, so they require little space and their roots fit easily into shallow trays.

Grow it vertically

The world's largest vertical farm is run by a company called AeroFarms, in Newark, New Jersey. A timed watering system sprays an aeroponic mist with the exact amount of water and nutrients required to grow a healthy plant, and LED lighting mimics the sun's rays. It's a closed system, which means no pests can get in, so there's no need for pesticides. Nutrients are recycled, and the whole system uses 95 percent less water than conventional farming.

Grow it on the roof

The city of Hong Kong, China, has over 300 skyscrapers, the most of any city in the world. Seven million people live in Hong Kong, and 72 percent of these high-rise buildings are residential. Could you imagine if each building was equipped with a rooftop farm capable of producing enough food to feed all of the people living in the building? You could take an elevator up to the roof, pick what you need for dinner, and be eating a fresh *zero-mile meal* minutes later. Yes, please!

The Sun Works greenhouse in New York City is part farm and part laboratory. Children visit the greenhouse on school trips to learn where their food comes from, how it's grown and why it's important—not a bad classroom!
ERICA GANNETT

If you don't have much yard space to grow food, reclaiming a pallet is a perfect way to build a micro garden.
ALISTAIR BERG /GETTY IMAGES

Rooftop gardens don't only provide food; they also purify the air and buffer temperatures. Unlike us, plants breathe in *carbon dioxide* and exhale oxygen. They are natural air purifiers armed to combat city smog, and they absorb the sun's rays, leaving the surfaces below them cool. On regular rooftops the sunshine is absorbed or reflected, adding to what's called the "urban heat island" effect, where a city is significantly warmer than its surrounding rural areas due to human activities. Have you ever heard of someone frying an egg on the sidewalk on a very hot day? It's a fun experiment, but it shows how hot artificial surfaces can get. In France, new legislation is making green space or solar panels mandatory on the roofs of all new commercial building developments.

Singapore imports over 90 percent of its vegetables, so making the most use of urban space by creating vertical food gardens is important to establishing food independence. SKYGREENS

URBAN HOMESTEADING

As we found out in Chapter 2, rural homesteaders try to make or source their own food, water, shelter, heat and clothing. Can you imagine trying to pull off this lifestyle in the city? You never know, your neighbors could be urban homesteaders!

Children at this inner-city school in Newark, NJ, get to eat their lunch beside a small vertical garden that supplies the dining hall with fresh greens—now that's zero mile! AEROFARMS

Chew on This!

If you like setting up a lemonade or iced tea stand in front of your house in the heat of summer, next time try making your stand mobile. Quiet streets may not have much foot traffic, so be like a food truck operator and go where people gather. Store your cool drinks in leak-proof thermoses designed to carry a large amount of liquid and ice. Look for ones with a spout on the bottom so you can pour drinks easily into cups. Otherwise you can open the top of the thermos and use a ladle. Load the thermoses and cups into a wagon and set up shop at a busy soccer field, baseball diamond or tennis court. You can offer people lemonade on your way to the game, at the game and on your way home—if you have any left!

Homesteaders always have conservation on the mind, especially when it comes to water. Rain barrels and a rainwater capture system are essential, but it's also a good idea to think up ways to make use of water after it's already been used. Instead of sending gray water (the water left after doing dishes, bathing or washing clothes) down the drain, some choose to repurpose it in toilets, or get really creative and use oyster mushrooms to filter the gray water for safe use in the garden and even to drink. Making use of gray water is kind of like bringing your reusable grocery bags with you when you shop, or remembering to turn off the lights when you leave a room. Every time you repurpose gray water, you conserve the Earth's supply of fresh water.

FOOD TRUCK FEVER

In 1872 an American named Walter Scott created a food cart out of a small horse-drawn wagon and sold food to people outside their workplaces. Today's food trucks are direct descendents of that original idea. Most city dwellers eat meals on the go, and for those who eat out for at least one meal every day, food trucks serve restaurant-quality food in a fraction of the time (and at a fraction of the price). They have become so popular you can find mobile street food the world over.

FARMING FACT: In the late 1700s a Frenchman named Nicolas Appert made the first canned food using sealed bottles. Soon after, food was being preserved for military rations in the tin cans we see today, but the first can opener wasn't invented until the 1860s, when non-military folk, like homesteaders, became interested in canned foods.

Hungry customers wait in line at this food truck in Victoria, BC. KIMBERLEY VENESS

Street food isn't always a cooked, grab-and-go meal. Some vendors serve fresh fruit!
TANAWAT PONTCHOUR/DREAMSTIME.COM

From Farm to Table

I met Aidan Pine one summer while working at a farmers' market. In the course of a year, his family farm went from raising 20 chickens to 200 to keep up with orders at the truck, and that was just the poultry. All the produce, lamb, pork and chicken he serves from his food truck come from the farm. It isn't unusual for Aidan to serve 50 pounds of beets in one week. People can't get enough of his farm-fresh flavors!

Chef Aidan Pine started his own food truck, called Juma, to serve local, sustainable and humanely raised food to urbanites in Victoria, BC.
SOL KAUFFMAN

CHAPTER FOUR

A Farm for the Future

DINNER'S IN THE FISH TANK

When you raise fish and vegetables together in the same system, it's called *aquaponics*. Fish live in a tank and the plants grow in soilless garden beds. Water is drawn from the fish tank to the plant beds by a pump and circulates through the growth medium. A pipe brings excess water back to the fish tank, aerating the water.

Setting up a small aquaponics system is fairly simple. A 75-liter (20-gallon) tank could support a few fish and provide a tomato plant with the nutrients it needs. Larger tanks can house larger fish like tilapia, trout, carp and largemouth bass—all popular edible species that do well in aquaponics. Goldfish and koi do well too, but are inedible. Eating fish you have raised yourself is half the fun of aquaponics, so raising edible varieties makes sense. It's a good idea to research how much space the type of fish will need before buying a tank.

This 4,500-square-metre aquaponics structure in the United Arab Emirates produces 40 tonnes of tilapia a year. The water is filtered and recirculated, and waste is treated and removed for use as fertilizer. In their first year they grew ninety-eight different plant cultivars on a huge piece of Styrofoam floating on the water.
PAUL VAN DER WERF

INSECTS...YUM!

Entomophagy is just a fancy word for eating insects. Two billion people eat insects every day. Street vendors serve up scorpions shish-kebab style, ants are coated in chocolate and crickets are fried to the perfect crunch and set out as snack food. For the most part, it's only in developed countries that people have an aversion to eating any of the close to 2,000 edible bug species.

In Japan, the larvae of yellow jacket wasps, known as *hebo*, are such a prized food there is a Hebo Festival each year to celebrate it. Raising insects for an alternative source of protein takes far less space, energy, water and feed than raising meat animals like cattle. One dairy cow produces about 54 kilograms (120 pounds) of manure a day; the waste insects make is tiny. For these reasons, some people are trying to bring entomophagy mainstream in creative ways, by making things like cricket flour you can use in baking.

In Cameroon, women forage for beetle larvae by pressing their ears to trees and listening for the sound of the larvae. When they hear something, they peel away the bark and harvest the larvae. Insects are an important food source in Africa during the rainy season, when finding other food is more challenging. Would you prefer to eat your bugs raw, sautéed or deep-fried?

In Mexico, a recipe of crunchy fried crickets is called chapulines and is loved by locals. This isn't a new food fad—Latin Americans have eaten this type of cricket for centuries.
ESDELVAL /ISTOCK.COM

FARMING FACT: Rainbow carrots are a colorful change from the regular orange carrots we're used to, but purple and white were the originals—the orange variety was bred later.

GREEN EGGS AND JELLYFISH

We have altered plant and animal genes through selective breeding since the start of agriculture 8,000 to 10,000 years ago. Now many see *genetic engineering (GE)* as a promising option to boost food production for future generations. Scientists alter the genes of plant and animal species in the lab to make them immune to chemical sprays, or to reduce the need for spraying in the field. The results of GE are called *genetically modified organisms (GMOS)*. Seventy-five percent of the non-organic processed foods we enjoy contain GE ingredients.

Chew on This!

RYAN LAUZE

Want to cut down on how much meat you eat but don't want to give it up altogether? Pick a day of the week, avoid eating meat for the whole day, and stick to it every week. Even this small action can have a big effect if you share what you're doing and why you're doing it with other people—they may feel inspired to do the same.

FARMING FACT: Average global meat consumption is 90 pounds per person per year. This fluctuates depending on country—one person in Australia or the United States could eat up to 120 kilograms (265 pounds) per year.

When the genes of two different animal species are merged, the result is called a *transgenic* organism. A joint research team in Australia and the United States is now looking into placing a green fluorescence (a form of luminescence) from a jellyfish into a sex chromosome of a chicken so that the chicken's sex is recognizable before the eggs hatch. Some believe this would be a breakthrough because the poultry industry only raises hens. There has been no long-term study on GE foods and human health, so advances in GE technology are still controversial.

LAB BURGER, ANYONE?

In 2013, scientists served the first lab-grown hamburger to a panel of taste testers. Their verdict? The texture was realistic, but it needed salt. The cultured beef patty was made by extracting muscle cells from a live cow, creating stem cells (cells that can create more of the same kind of cell), adding collagen (animal protein) and watching under a microscope as the connective tissue formed. Those who believe lab burgers could save the meat industry say the beef is way safer to eat than feedlot meat; there is no risk of unknowingly consuming growth hormones and antibiotics, getting sick from *E. coli* or mad cow disease, or developing higher susceptibility for health problems.

Can you imagine a world where the majority of meat was artificially created in petri dishes and test tubes? It may seem extreme, but the feed, energy and water conventional farming requires, as well as its toxic outputs and dangers to human health, make lab meat not a bad option for satisfying people's taste for meat in the future. We would just have to get past the yuck factor, and that could take a few generations!

MILK: BEYOND THE CEREAL BOWL

In 2010, researchers in Buenos Aires, Argentina, genetically engineered a transgenic cow named Rosita ISA. The cow was the first to produce two human proteins in its milk: lactoferrin and lysozyme, an antibody that fights illness and infection. Both proteins occur naturally in breast milk and are important for infant health. In 2012, scientists successfully created a cow whose milk was hypoallergenic, meaning people allergic to milk could drink it and not have an allergic reaction!

GE technology is still very new. Experiments are mostly trial and error, which means most transgenic animals die soon after birth. While the research is being done to meet our needs, it's important to remember that humans are animals too. Those opposed to transgenic research believe tampering with another animal's life to achieve our own ambitions is unjust.

Born in 1997, Dolly the sheep was the first mammal successfully cloned from an adult cell.
TONI BARROS/WIKIPEDIA.ORG

FARMING FACT: Field corn is used to make animal feed, corn flour and processed foods like tortilla chips. Sweet corn is the type you eat off the cob. Most field corn is GE.

From Farm to Table

My dad was a hunter, so aside from the chickens and cows we raised on our farm, much of the meat in my family's diet came from wild animals like deer, elk and moose. He went on hunting trips a couple of times each year, so we had a steady supply of meat in our freezer. Sometimes my brothers and sisters and I would walk around our acreage with our dad, tracking smaller game like wild rabbit and pheasant, and scanning the sky for Canada goose.

My dad circa 1997 with a whitetail buck.
KIMBERLEY VENESS

Four young boys walking in a rice field, in Sa Pa, Northern Vietnam. ONFOKUS/ISTOCK.COM

REVOLUTIONARY RICE?

Every mammal species produces milk to feed its offspring. The milk each species makes has been finely tuned to have the specific amount of vitamins, fat, protein and carbohydrates the babies require.
CHELSEA WARREN

Did you know that all rice is brown when harvested? It only turns white after processing in a rice polisher, a machine that buffs the brown bran layer and leaves the endosperm (white carbohydrate) we recognize as white rice. White rice has a much longer shelf life than brown rice, but the bran layer holds the majority of nutrients, making brown rice higher in fiber, oils, B vitamins and minerals. If stored in an airtight container in a cool, dry place, white rice has an infinite shelf life. Brown, on the other hand, will last only three to six months in your pantry because of its intact layer of oil—but think of all those yummy vitamins!

The first prototype for GE rice came out in 2000. If successful, this "golden rice" would contain high levels of beta-carotene (which is converted to vitamin A in the human body) inside the endosperm. Vitamin A is very important for healthy vision, growth and immune system function. Some believe that golden rice is a good candidate for improving health in developing countries, while others argue that genetically engineering crops over-complicates the prevalent global problem of making healthy foods accessible and affordable for everyone.

BEE BIZ

Thousands of bee species buzz around the world, and while not every species makes honey, they are all equally important pollinators. If bees vanished, we would lose one third of all fruits, nuts and vegetables grown worldwide.

The RoboBee is about the size of a raspberry, and its wings beat 120 times per second.
KEVIN MA & PAKPONG CHIRARATTANANON/WIKIPEDIA.ORG

Bees are used on a mass scale to pollinate huge monoculture fields of crops, like almonds. To ensure maximum pollination, bee brokers transport bees in semi-trucks to the fields and set down the hives beside the road. The bees do their work, return to their hives and are trucked to the next field. Bee populations are in decline, and though many people are still divided on the reason why, research indicates the culprit may be insecticide sprayed on crops.

Now scientists are using *biomimicry* (creating technologies to mimic processes in nature) to manufacture the RoboBee, a miniature robot they hope can pollinate crops if we lose the bees. The potential for helpful robotic bees is exciting, but scientists hope they never have to replace bees altogether.

New LED lights cast a pinkish hue on the plants in the Mars-Lunar Greenhouse.

GENE GIACOMELLI/PHOTO COURTESY OF PHILIPS LIGHTING.

Organic vegetables at a weekly farmers' market in Santa Barbara, CA, USA.

CSFOTOIMAGES/ISTOCK.COM

FARMING IN SPACE!

Antarctica is a perfect place to experiment with how we would go about growing food on another planet. The continent experiences four months of continuous light and four months of continuous dark, separated by four months of sunlight resembling dawn or dusk. This variance in sunlight, and freezing conditions, makes agriculture impossible unless done indoors under controlled conditions.

Shipping soil to Antarctica is prohibited because of the risk of transmission of invasive soil microbes, so researchers at the South Pole grow vegetables and fruit using hydroponics to provide a reliable supply of year-round fresh produce. The South Pole Food Growth Chambers' success led to the development of the Prototype Lunar Greenhouse. It's lightweight and collapsible, perfect for packing into a rocket and launching to another planet.

People from around the world are now being selected to take a one-way trip to Mars in 2030 to form the first human colony on another planet. To ensure a reliable supply of oxygen, food and water for our first colony, systems would need to repurpose 100 percent of water and waste in a closed-loop system. Some researchers think the diet would be strictly vegetarian because of lack of space and feed requirements for livestock, but it might be possible to raise insects for extra protein.

BRINGING IT BACK TO THE TABLE

Regardless of where you live, opportunities exist to connect with the foods you enjoy. All food, whether it's an apple, a yam, an egg or a steak, has a story to tell about where it came from and under what conditions it was raised. Whether you cut down on eating beef, make your own butter or pitch in at a commons garden, there are plenty of things that you can do to help make our world's food system more sustainable now and for future generations.

People have shared meals together for thousands of years, making the family dinner table a great spot to catch up with loved ones and continue the tradition.
JENNY ACHESON/GETTY IMAGES

Resources

Books

Berners-Lee, Mike. *How Bad Are Bananas? The Carbon Footprint of Everything.* Vancouver: Greystone Books, 2011.

Mulder, Michelle. *Every Last Drop: Bringing Clean Water Home.* Victoria: Orca Book Publishers, 2014.

Standage, Tom. *An Edible History of Humanity.* London, UK: Atlantic Books, 2010.

Tate, Nikki. *Down to Earth: How Kids Help Feed the World.* Victoria: Orca Book Publishers, 2013.

Taub-Dix, Bonnie. *Read It Before You Eat It: How to Decode Food Labels and Make the Healthiest Choice Every Time.* New York: Plume, 2010.

Wilcox, Merrie-Ellen. *What's the Buzz? Keeping Bees in Flight.* Victoria: Orca Book Publishers, 2015.

Websites

Environmental Working Group: www.ewg.org

Food and Agriculture Organization of the United Nations: www.fao.org

National Geographic Food Series: food.nationalgeographic.com

SeaChoice: www.seachoice.org

World Watch Institute: www.worldwatch.org

World Wide Opportunities on Organic Farms: www.wwoof.net

Videos

Earthlight Documentary:
http://cals.arizona.edu/earthlight/videos

Food by the Numbers: Feeding Our Hungry Planet:
http://video.nationalgeographic.com/video/food-by-the-numbers/141014-world-food-day-ngfood?source=searchvideo

Soils: Our Ally Against Climate Change:
https://www.youtube.com/watch?v=8_69vy7ZBxE

Acknowledgments

I would first like to thank my late brother, Matthew. Without witnessing his meticulous passion for writing fiction, I probably wouldn't have given writing a try and realized it was a career I was interested in pursuing. Thank you to my parents, Kim and Lisbeth, for risking it all and taking a chance on building a life on an acreage—in the middle of Saskatchewan, no less. Those years shaped my personality, my interests and my ambitions. Thank you, David Leach, for your mentorship with *Concrete Garden*. Thank you, Anne Mullens. You have been a mentor, confidant and friend. Your skill with writing, your energy while teaching, and your unwavering compassion are a constant inspiration to me.

I would like to thank Orca Book Publishers for signing my first book. Sustainable agriculture is close to my heart, and I'm thrilled to have been able to tell just a few of the stories of how people are growing food around the world. Thank you, Sarah Harvey and Jenn Playford, for your guidance and advice. My hunt for pictures connected me with artists, photographers, entrepreneurs and businesses all over the world, from Canada to the United States, Argentina, the Netherlands, Africa, Antarctica and more. Thank you to everyone who allowed me to use their pictures in this book.

I would like to thank my mother-in-law, Laura Carbonneau, for supporting me throughout the final stages of my book writing, taking Landon on adventures and continually putting my mind at ease. Thank you to my best friend, Sarah Sabo. Those Skype calls kept me sane! Finally, I'd like to thank my partner, Ryan Lauze, for getting up in the middle of the night, letting me sleep in as long as I pleased, and keeping the coffee going on the days I had to binge write. Thank you!

Glossary

aeroponics—the process of growing plants without the use of soil or a growing medium

animal by-products—any material derived from an animal that is not directly intended for human consumption

aquaponics—any system in which aquatic animals are raised in tanks with plants in an environment that benefits both the plants and animals

biomimicry—creating technologies to mimic processes in nature

biosolids—processed human sewage

carbon dioxide (CO2)—a gas produced when people and animals breathe out or when certain fuels are burned; it is used by plants for energy

certified organic—a label for food grown without using synthetic pesticides or fertilizers, growth hormones, antibiotics and animal by-products, and is not a GMO

chemical fertilizers—any natural or synthetic material that is refined to its pure chemical state and then applied to soils or to plant tissues to supply nutrients essential to the growth of plants

commons gardens—gardens maintained by community volunteers; can be harvested by all residents

community gardens—large areas of discrete garden plots that are maintained and harvested by individual gardeners

companion planting—planting different crops in proximity to pest control, to promote pollination, provide habitat for beneficial creatures, maximize use of space, and otherwise increase crop productivity

Concentrated Animal Feeding Operations (CAFOs)—a food production process that concentrates large numbers of animals in relatively small and confined places

contamination—the process of making something dangerous, dirty or impure by directly or indirectly adding something harmful or undesirable to it

ecosystem—an intricate system where everything that exists in a particular environment relies on the other parts of that environment in some way

entomophagy—the human consumption of insects as food environmental regulations—rules that companies and organizations must follow to help prevent pollution and to protect the environment and human health

export commodity—a good or service that is produced in one country, then shipped to others for distribution and sale abroad

feedlot—a plot of land on which livestock are fattened for market

food desert—an area where affordable and nutritious food is hard to obtain, particularly for those without access to an automobile

food forest (also known as a forest garden)—a permaculture landscape based on woodland ecosystems in which every plant produces something useful to humans at different times of the year

food miles—the distance food is transported before it reaches the consumer. Food miles are one factor used when assessing the environmental impact of agriculture

genetic engineering (GE)—the modification of an organism's genetic composition by artificial means, often involving the transfer of specific traits, or genes, from one organism into a plant or animal of an entirely different species

genetically modified organisms (GMOs)—organisms that have been modified through genetic engineering in an attempt to improve or change them, often called transgenic

growth hormones—a chemical messenger in the body that stimulates growth in animal or plant cells

herbivorous—an animal that only eats plants

hydroponics—a method of growing plants using mineral nutrient solutions in water or other growing mediums besides soil

Industrial Revolution—the transition to new manufacturing processes that involved replacing human labor with machines and took place from 1760 to sometime between 1820 and 1840

integrated rice and duck farming—using ducks to eliminate weeds and pests in rice fields

invertebrates—animals without a backbone

lasagna gardening—stacking layers of compostable scraps, coffee grounds, leaves, straw and newspaper clippings on top of the soil to enrich it

monocultures—single crops grown on large areas of land

omnivorous—an animal that eats both plants and other animals

pasteurization—a process where a product is heated up to extend shelf life and kill harmful bacteria before being sold for human consumption, as with milk and other dairy products

pathogen—a virus, bacteria or other microorganism that causes disease

permaculture—the creation of sustainable, self-sufficient ecosystems for the long term, requiring less input of chemical pesticides, water and human labor, and resulting in less output of greenhouse gases

pesticide—a chemical that is used to kill animals or insects that damage plants or crops

tilling—using hand tools or machinery to dig, stir or overturn soil in preparation for planting.

transgenic—a term used to describe a genetically modified organism

zero-mile meal—a meal produced from ingredients grown or raised in the same location as they are eaten

Index

Index (continued)